Y0-DBV-438

Marie Curie
Angela Bull

Illustrated by
Edward Mortelmans

Hamish Hamilton
London

Titles in the Profiles *series*

HAMISH HAMILTON CHILDREN'S BOOKS

Penguin Books Ltd, 27 Wrights Lane, London W8 5TZ (Publishing & Editorial)
and Harmondsworth, Middlesex, England (Distribution & Warehouse)
Viking Penguin Inc., 40 West 23rd Street, New York, New York 10010, U.S.A.
Penguin Books Australia Ltd, Ringwood, Victoria, Australia
Penguin Books Canada Limited, 2801 John Street, Markham, Ontario, Canada L3R 1B4
Penguin Books (N.Z.) Ltd, 182 – 190 Wairau Road, Auckland 10, New Zealand

First published in Great Britain 1986 by
Hamish Hamilton Children's Books

Copyright © 1986 text by Angela Bull
Copyright © 1986 illustrations by Edward Mortelmans

Reprinted 1987

British Library Cataloguing in Publication Data

Bull, Angela
Marie Curie. — (Profiles)
1. Curie, Marie — Juvenile literature
2. Chemists — France — Biography
I. Title   II. Series
540'.92'4   QD22.C8

ISBN 0-241-11741-0

Typeset by Pioneer
Printed in Great Britain at the
University Press, Cambridge

Contents

Little Marya Sklodovska in her father's study

1 A Polish Family

Marie Curie became famous as a scientist living and working in France; but she was born in Poland, and when she was a child she had a Polish name — Marya Sklodovska.

*   *   *

Little Marya peeped round the open door of her father's study. The room was empty, so she tiptoed in.

Papa's study was full of attractive things. Besides the big, tidy desk, there were red plush armchairs, a shiny green clock, and a barometer hanging on the wall. But Marya hurried past them all to the cabinet in the far corner. This was her favourite thing, and, flattening her nose against the glass door, she stared at the fascinating objects inside — test-tubes, tiny weighing scales, mysterious crystals in jars.

Suddenly she heard her father's tread. Into the room came Professor Sklodovski, a plump, bearded man, wearing a neat, dark suit.

'Papa,' Marya exclaimed, 'what are the things in this cabinet?'

'Apparatus for physics,' he answered.

For some reason the words delighted Marya. She repeated them slowly. 'Apparatus for physics. Apparatus for physics.'

'These are for weighing very precisely,' said Papa, stooping down beside her, and pointing to the scales. 'And this is an electroscope. I can use it to detect electrical charges.'

Madame Sklodovska

'Do you use it for lessons?' Marya asked.

Professor Sklodovski shook his head.

'Not now,' he said sadly. 'There isn't time. We have to teach Russian instead of science.'

Marya had been born in the Polish city of Warsaw on 7 November 1867, just three years after the Poles had rebelled against the Russians who ruled their country. The rebellion failed; Russian control became even tighter. Warsaw children were made to spend long hours studying Russian. Other subjects, like physics, had to be abandoned.

Both Marya's parents were descended from families who had once helped to govern Poland, and fight for its freedom. One of her uncles had been a leader in the recent uprising, and an aunt had organized a secret hospital where freedom fighters were treated before they were smuggled out of the country. But though Marya's parents were patriotic, they were not fighters. They were quiet, scholarly people, devoted to education.

Marya's mother had been a headmistress. All her children — Sophie, Joseph, Bronya, Helen and Marya — were born in the flat above her school. When Marya was one, Mrs Sklodovska became ill, and her husband persuaded her to give up working. The family moved to the boys' school where Professor Sklodovski taught, and here they were given rooms in a back wing. Marya grew up to the sound of clanging bells, the smell of chalk and ink, and the sight of shelves full of books.

In such surroundings, and with such parents, the Sklodovski children were naturally studious; but little Marya soon began to show signs of unusual brilliance. As a tiny child she played with the cardboard letters from which her elder sister, Bronya, was learning the alphabet, and, by herself, she mastered their meaning. One day, when Bronya was struggling over a reading lesson with her mother, Marya reached out, took the book, and began to read aloud. On and on she went, until suddenly she noticed Bronya's scowl, and the astonished expressions of her parents. Not realizing how clever she had been, and afraid they might blame

Marya reading at an early age

her for showing off, she burst into tears.

'I didn't do it on purpose,' she sobbed. 'It was so easy.'

Marya hated upsetting her sisters. She thought they were wonderful, and very pretty, with their lively faces and long fair hair. She herself was rather plain, a small, plump, snub-nosed child with unruly yellow curls.

In their back rooms the children worked and played together. They were expected to keep very quiet, and not only during lesson times. The headmaster, a Russian whom they secretly nicknamed the 'Ogre', was a severe, unfriendly man, who demanded silence, even at week-ends. The children were afraid of him, and, when they dared to play outside, they always crept noiselessly past his windows. They knew he disliked his Polish teachers, and for their father's sake, as well as their own, they did not want to annoy him.

Something else, besides life in the school, made the children subdued. Although it was seldom mentioned, they could not help knowing that their mother was ill. They noticed her pale face, and the cough that never went away. Mrs Sklodovska had tuberculosis, a disease for which there was no cure in those days. She was so desperately anxious not to spread the infection, that she never hugged or kissed her children. She worked for them, and prayed for them, but she kept them at arm's length.

For love, Marya turned to her brother and sisters. Joseph was always studying, and Helen was absorbed in music, so that Marya's closest companion was Bronya. But above all she adored Sophie, seven years older than herself, and a clever, charming girl, who mothered all the family.

Their quiet life in the boys' school lasted until Marya was six, and then the first blow fell. The Russian headmaster, who had always distrusted Professor Sklodovski, picked a quarrel with him, cut his salary, and turned the family out of their rooms. Suddenly they were homeless, and almost penniless. As they moved from one cheap flat to another, it was Sophie's courage which helped everyone to be brave, and Sophie's warmth which made the most dismal surroundings into a home.

The children tiptoeing past the headmaster's study

Mrs Sklodovska's health broke down under the strain. Somehow enough money was scraped together for her to spend a winter in the south of France, away from the freezing cold of Warsaw. But she could not look after herself, and, to Marya's dismay, she took Sophie with her. All through the winter, Marya counted the days until Sophie came back.

Blow was to follow blow. Hardly had the travellers returned in the spring, with Mrs Sklodovska still thin and frail, than Sophie and Bronya caught typhus fever. Marya was forbidden to see them. She only knew that, behind their closed bedroom door, they were seriously ill. There was a flicker of hope when Bronya began to recover, but then terrible news was broken to the other children. Sophie had died. For the last time they saw her, white and beautiful in her coffin, and then she was carried away for burial.

Marya was eight when she lost Sophie, and ten when her mother finally died, whispering 'I love you' to the children she had not kissed for years. Forlorn and shaken, Marya and Bronya, Joseph and Helen, clung together in a Warsaw flat which did not feel at all like home.

2 School-Days and Holidays

For some time now Bronya, Helen and Marya had been pupils at Miss Sikorska's private school. They set off every morning in their blue uniform dresses, their hair tied neatly back. At least, Bronya's and Helen's hair was neat. Marya's yellow curls always escaped from their plait.

All Warsaw schools were directed by the government to give a Russian-based education, but Miss Sikorska was a secret rebel. At her school there were lessons in Polish history and literature, given in Polish. Russian inspectors constantly toured the schools, but Miss Sikorska knew how to outwit them. When an inspector appeared at the school gate, the porter pressed a hidden bell, so that two long peals and two short ones sounded in the classrooms. The Polish books were whisked into hiding places, and the inspector found only rows of girls sewing, while their teachers read aloud in Russian.

Law-abiding though they looked, they were not left in peace. Each visit meant an examination, with the inspector firing Russian questions at the pupils, to make sure they were learning the right things. Marya, unfortunately, was the best at Russian in her class. Time after time Miss Sikorska asked her to stand up, and answer the hated inspector.

'Who is your ruler?' he would demand.

'His Majesty Alexander II, Tsar of all the Russias,' Marya was obliged to reply.

As a final humiliation at the end of each visit, the inspector made the girls recite the Lord's Prayer in

A Russian school inspector

Russian. It seemed that they could not even observe their religion in their own way.

Since no one knew when the inspector would arrive, the atmosphere at school was tense and jumpy; and when Marya and her sisters reached home, things were not much better. To make ends meet, Professor Sklodovski had rented a large flat where he could take pupils from his school as boarders, offering them extra lessons for extra payment. Sometimes as many as ten noisy, romping, boys were squeezed into the flat, and the girls had to sleep in the dining-room.

A plain tea was ready when they got in from school,

and then it was time for homework. This was hard, for every subject had to be studied in Russian. Bronya and Helen sighed and dawdled, but Marya sat down at once, and, with her elbows on the table, lost herself in study. She had great powers of concentration, and an amazingly accurate memory. Nothing was too difficult for her. At the age of ten, she was in a class with girls of twelve.

Perhaps her cleverness was a little irritating, for one day her sisters and a cousin decided to play a trick on her. As she read, they piled chairs in a tower over and around her. For half-an-hour Marya worked on without noticing. Then she closed her book, sat up — and chairs crashed in every direction.

'How silly!' Marya remarked scornfully.

When she was not actually studying, Marya read everything she could find — poetry, adventure stories, and scientific books. Reading was the best escape from her difficult life. Her father encouraged her, and on Saturday evening, as a special treat, he read aloud to all the children.

Presently, because Bronya and Marya were so clever, he moved them to a Russian state school. Here standards were much higher than at Miss Sikorska's, and discipline much stricter. Marya was often in trouble for her untidy hair. There were Russian and German, as well as Polish girls at the school, but the national groups kept rigidly apart. The Polish girls would not even speak to the Russians, and they behaved as rebelliously as they dared. The teachers were furious when some Polish girls, including Marya, were found

Marya praying for the life of her friend's brother

dancing for joy in their classroom because Tsar Alexander had been murdered. It was a brave thing to do, for the girls were well aware of how dangerous their Russian rulers could be. The brother of one of Marya's friends was sentenced to death for being involved in a plot against the government in Warsaw. Marya stayed up all through the night before the execution, praying with her friend.

It was a point of honour among the Polish girls to hate school, and Marya was ashamed to admit openly that she liked it — but she did. She loved studying, even in Russian. When, at the early age of sixteen, she finished her school course, she won the gold medal for the best student, and a pile of Russian prize books. But

19

Horse riding in the country

she had been under too much of a strain with the hard work and tension at school, the turmoil at home, and the lingering grief for her mother and Sophie. As her school-days ended, Marya suffered a kind of nervous collapse.

The cure the doctors suggested was a year's holiday. Professor Sklodovski sent Marya south from Warsaw on a round of visits to relations in the country. Marya loved their open-air life. She learned to ride, swim and climb mountains. 'I can't believe that algebra and geometry ever existed,' she wrote home. 'I have forgotten them completely.'

While staying with an uncle and aunt, Marya took part in a *kulig*. This was a traditional Polish celebration, and very exciting. Marya and her cousins, in peasant costumes, set off through the snow in a sleigh, with young men riding beside them carrying flaming torches. Converging with other sleighs, they arrived at a big house where music was playing. They rushed in to dance waltzes and mazurkas, until, at a sudden signal, they climbed back into the sleighs, and sped on to another house, where the music began again. For three days they travelled and danced, with only brief pauses to sleep in barns full of hay. In every house the tables were laden with food and wine, and there was joking, singing and flirting. It seemed very far from grim, Russian-dominated Warsaw.

Marya returned home plump and well. Things had improved. The schoolboy boarders had gone, and the family had moved to a nicer house. Bronya looked after it, Joseph was a medical student, and Helen was studying music. The question facing seventeen-year-old Marya was what she should do next.

3 The Young Governess

After a year away from her books, Marya was longing to study again. Joseph was at Warsaw University, and how she envied him! Sadly for her, Polish universities expected their students to know Latin and Greek, which were not taught in girls' schools. It was a Russian way of preventing girls from having further education.

But, Bronya told Marya, there was a way, a secret way. In Warsaw itself there was a 'floating university'. All over the city, groups of people were meeting in each other's houses for an education which the Russians knew nothing about. Polish intellectuals had realized that, although they might never be strong enough to fight for political freedom, they must keep their cultural heritage alive. If people remembered Polish history and literature, they would not easily be submerged in the vast Russian empire.

Marya went eagerly with Bronya to her first class at the 'floating university'. Most of the students were teenage girls and young women, friendly and lively, and so keen to improve their education that they were willing to risk exile in Siberia, which might be their punishment if the Russians caught them. Marya studied natural history, anatomy and sociology; she read widely in French, German and Russian as well as Polish; she learned to enjoy intellectual arguments; and she shared with other students an idealistic belief that, in the future, all human problems would be solved through science. She hurried from class to class, burning with new ideas.

Reading aloud to working girls

One of the aims of the 'floating university' was to spread a knowledge of Polish literature. Marya had got to know some girls who worked for a dressmaker, and she began to make time to read aloud to them, and to collect Polish books for them to borrow. But as her enthusiasm grew, Bronya's was beginning to fade.

Bronya was tired of half measures. Ever since she left school she had kept house for the family, and mothered her brother and sisters, as Sophie had once done. Now she was twenty, and she wanted more out of life than housework, and classes at the 'floating university'. She wanted to train as a doctor, as Joseph was doing. And since she could not study in Warsaw, she dreamed of going to Paris. By giving private lessons in her spare time she had earned enough money to pay for her fare to France, and a year's training; but the medical course lasted five years, and how would she ever save enough for it all?

Marya saw her sister's despair, and she had a brilliant idea. Bronya could go straight to Paris and begin the course; and she herself would take a job as a governess, sending all the money she earned to Bronya, to pay for the rest of the training. When Bronya finished, she, in her turn, could use her doctor's salary to provide a university education for Marya.

Delightfully simple as the plan was, Bronya felt uneasy. Marya was far cleverer than she was; surely she should be the one to go to Paris. Marya disagreed. Bronya must go first as she was the elder. 'When you have your medical practice,' said Marya, 'you can bury me in gold – in fact, I shall count on it.'

So Bronya left for Paris, and Marya looked for a post as a governess. With her gold medal, and her knowledge of several languages, she was well qualified; and she was soon travelling north to the village of Szczuki, where she had been engaged to teach ten-year-old Andzia Zorawska.

A journey by train and sleigh brought Marya, late in the evening, to an old-fashioned, gabled house, covered with creepers, where she received a kind welcome from the Zorawski family. Szczuki was in the country, she had heard, and she looked forward to enjoying country pleasures again. When she looked out of her window in

The Zorawski family home

the morning, she was dreadfully disappointed. She could see nothing but huge, flat fields of sugar-beet, stretching in every direction, without trees or hedges, while beside the house stood a smoky factory, where the beet was refined into sugar.

For Bronya's sake she threw herself into her work. She liked the Zorawskis. Besides Andzia and an older girl, there were two little ones at home, and some boys away at school and university. In the evenings Marya worked by herself. She borrowed scientific books from the factory, and sat up late studying physics and chemistry. Often she sighed for a laboratory, where she could try experiments for herself. Learning science from books was very unsatisfactory. When she was tired

Boating with Casimir

of reading, she relaxed over maths problems, which she sent to her father to be corrected.

She had not forgotten the ideals of the 'floating university', and presently she saw a chance of putting them into practice. The workers at the sugar-beet factory lived in a dreary little village with no school for the children. Marya began to give them evening lessons in her bedroom. At first the children came reluctantly. They were dirty, ignorant, and inattentive. But Marya persevered, and after a while the parents too began crowding into the bedroom, to stare in wonder as their children read aloud, and did simple sums.

Suddenly, and unexpectedly, romance broke into Marya's hard-working life. The eldest Zorawski son, Casimir, came home from Warsaw University, where he was studying science, and met his sister's clever young governess for the first time. Marya was thrilled to have the chance of talking to a scientist, but they found they shared more than intellectual interests. It was summer. Casimir liked outdoor activities, and he took Marya riding and boating with him. He was a good-looking young man, and Marya had grown much prettier. She was slim now. Her fair hair was smooth and thick, her eyes large and dreamy. She and Casimir fell in love.

Casimir in love with the governess! His parents were horrified. They hurried him back to the university, and told Marya never to speak to him again. Miserable and humiliated, Marya tried to forget him in longer hours of study, but her work seemed joyless. She hated the flat fields, the smoky factory, and the coldness with which the Zorawskis now treated her.

Fortunately rescue was near. Professor Sklodovski had taken a new job, with a higher salary. He wrote to say that he could pay the last part of Bronya's university fees. Marya could come home, and prepare for her own journey to Paris.

4 A Student in Paris

Marya's family expected her to rush to Paris at once. She was so clever, and she loved studying. What could be more attractive to her than life as a full-time student? Yet Marya seemed strangely reluctant.

She hesitated for several reasons. First, her father was now living by himself. She wondered if she should stay at home and keep him company. Then Joseph needed financial help to start his career as a doctor. Perhaps he should have the first claim on their father's money. She was doubtful too about leaving Poland. Would it mean betraying the ideals of the 'floating university' if she went to study abroad? Lastly she had met Casimir Zorawski again. Perhaps, most of all, she wanted to marry him, although it would mean a hard fight against his parents' opposition.

The arguments beat around inside her head. What should she do? Bronya, who was now engaged to a Polish medical student who was also living in Paris, wrote to Marya, urging her to come. She could offer Marya a room in her house as soon as she was married. Still Marya wavered.

What made her finally decide to go to Paris was a new experience, even more thrilling than a love affair. A cousin of hers was in charge of the so-called Warsaw Museum of Industry and Agriculture. The name was, in fact, a front to deceive the Russians, for the 'Museum' was really a laboratory, where science was taught, in Polish, to students of the 'floating university'.

Marya made her way there one Sunday afternoon,

The train journey across Europe

and suddenly memories of the old physics apparatus in her father's study came flooding back. She could hardly wait to handle scales and test-tubes at last. Standing at the bench, performing her first experiments in physics and chemistry, she knew, beyond a shadow of doubt, that this was what she wanted. Neither her father, nor her brother, nor even Casimir, really mattered. She must be a scientist.

In October 1891 she left Warsaw by train. For three days she rattled westward across Europe, perched on a folding chair in the middle of a fourth-class carriage, surrounded by her trunk, a rolled-up mattress, and bags crammed with food for the journey. At last she reached Paris, and there at the station was Bronya, with her new husband. As they hurried Marya to their flat, she stared around in amazement. She had never seen cars or electric lights before. But Bronya would not let her linger. She had a good, hot Polish meal waiting for her little sister.

Next morning Marya enrolled as a student. The University of Paris, the Sorbonne as it was called, was being rebuilt. Everything was chaotic. The laboratories were housed in makeshift huts. But to Marya it seemed marvellous. She applied for the physics course, signing herself for the first time as Marie Sklodovska. She had to be French now, not Polish.

Her first months in Paris were difficult. She had not realized that the French language would be a problem. She had been able to read French for years. But understanding the spoken French of the university lecturers was another matter. Often she could not follow them at all. Another disadvantage was the patchiness of her scientific knowledge. Because she had only read such books as she could get hold of, she knew nothing systematically. The French students seemed far ahead of her.

The solution to her problems was hard study, but here another difficulty arose. Bronya's flat was a centre for Polish exiles in Paris. They flocked in, to chatter and argue, and enjoy Bronya's excellent cooking. Revolutionary talk flowed over glasses of vodka and bowls of beetroot soup. But Marie had come to Paris for science, not politics. Before long she told Bronya she would have to move out. She needed peace and solitude to study properly.

She found herself a tiny attic room, lit by a skylight. It was furnished with a bed, a table, and a chair, and heated with a small stove, for which coal had to be carried up six flights of stairs. Yet in this stark setting, Marie was happier than she had ever been before. Physics fascinated her. Nothing could be more exciting,

Marie's attic room in Paris

she thought, than to discover the laws which governed the universe. They were stranger and more compelling than any novel or fairy-tale. For long hours she worked in the laboratories, performing her experiments with absolute precision, filling notebook after notebook with her neat writing and detailed diagrams. She was much too absorbed to bother about shopping and cooking for herself. The life of the mind was all that counted — until one day she fainted in class.

Another student summoned Marie's brother-in-law. He hurried to her attic, and found her lying on the bed, looking white, and very thin.

'What did you have for dinner last night?' he asked.

'Some cherries, and half a bunch of radishes.'

'What time did you go to bed?'

'Three o'clock this morning.'

'And you got up . . . ?'

'At seven.'

'Breakfast?'

'I didn't have any,' Marie admitted.

'Lunch?'

'The rest of the radishes.'

Her brother-in-law asked no more. He whisked Marie back to his flat, where Bronya restored her with steak and chips. But soon she was back in her attic, living as frugally as before.

In winter she was often frozen. Her clothes were inadequate; her shoes leaked. Once she was reduced to putting her chair on top of her scanty bedclothes in an attempt to gain some more warmth as she tried to sleep. But what did she care? Nothing mattered; nothing but science. As she worked she framed an ideal for herself. She would make scientific discoveries, not for the use they might have, or the fame they might bring her, but simply for their own sake. Pure knowledge would be her goal.

Her final exams came in 1893. She was so nervous she could hardly read the first question paper, but the familiar words were reassuring. She began to write, swiftly and neatly, covering sheet after sheet.

The results were announced in public to a huge assembly of students. Trembling, Marie took her seat. The professor began to read. 'Physics: first, Marie Sklodovska.' People stared in disbelief, and then burst into applause. After only two years in Paris, the foreign girl, who had been so badly handicapped by her imperfect French and her flawed scientific background, had come top of her year.

5 Pierre

Marie was certain now that she wanted to devote her life to physics. Only one thing held her back. Her knowledge of maths was as patchy as her knowledge of science had been, and physics depended a good deal on maths, since it was all about measuring and calculating natural phenomena, like electrical currents, energy, gravitational forces and acceleration. So she enrolled for the degree course in mathematics, and planned to complete it in one year.

At the same time she was asked by the French Society for the Encouragement of Industry to make a study for them of the magnetic properties of various steels; and, busy though she was, she agreed, for the subject interested her. She began the tests for magnetism in a laboratory at the Sorbonne; but there was not enough room for all her equipment and steel samples, so, wondering what to do, she turned for advice to another Polish scientist living in Paris. He remembered that a French physicist, Pierre Curie, had space in his laboratory at the Paris School of Physics and Chemistry, where he was a lecturer; he invited Marie to meet Pierre at his flat, to discuss possible arrangements.

Pierre Curie was eight years older than Marie, and already a distinguished scientist. He and his brother had discovered a method of compressing crystals to produce electricity, and had invented an electrometer, which could measure tiny currents with perfect accuracy. His brother was now a professor in the south of France. Pierre, left behind in Paris, had first

Pierre Curie

investigated the scientific principles of symmetry, and
then moved on to study magnetism. His approach to
science exactly matched Marie's. Because he believed
in the single-minded pursuit of knowledge, he had let
slip several chances of making money and gaining
promotion.

He was a tall, bearded man, with dreamy eyes, and
long, deft hands which could construct and operate
precision instruments. He was thin, and rather shabby,
because food and clothes did not interest him. Marie
liked him at once. She began explaining her research,
and asking questions about his; and he watched her,
noticing not only her clever, attractive face, but also
the untidy hair and acid-stained hands, which showed

that, like him, she was too busy with her work to care how she looked.

Eager to help her, and get to know her better, Pierre invited her to work at the Paris School of Physics and Chemistry. And he sent her a present; not flowers or chocolates, but a copy of his latest book, *On Symmetry in Physical Phenomena*. Marie found it enthralling. She asked him to visit her in her attic, and soon they were deeply in love.

One spring day Pierre took Marie to a fair at Sceaux, the little town near Paris where his parents lived. A whole day's holiday was unusual for them both, and

Pierre visiting Marie in her attic

they were enjoying themselves when a crowd of gaily-dressed peasants suddenly swept them apart, and for a few moments they lost each other. Pierre felt a stab of panic, a strange certainty that their whole relationship would end with just such terrifying abruptness, and he could not bear the thought.

He began to implore her to marry him. Marie did not know what to say. She felt sure that she ought to go back to Poland after her mathematics exam, and use her education for the good of her country. Pierre disagreed. He pointed out that there were no proper facilities for research in Warsaw. 'You can't abandon science now,' he urged; meaning as well, 'you can't abandon me.'

All through the summer of 1894 Marie tried to make up her mind. Of course she loved Pierre. As a husband he would suit her perfectly, and she knew that both his parents and Bronya wanted her to marry him. But she could not easily give up the ideals of the 'floating university'. Such was the turmoil in her mind that, in the examinations for the maths degree, she came only second, not first. By now it hardly mattered. When the results were announced, she immediately left Paris for Warsaw. Perhaps she would be able to think more clearly at home, away from Pierre.

That, at least, was her hope, but day after day letters arrived from Pierre. She could not change the political state of Poland, he told her, but she could change the course of science if she returned to Paris and worked with him. If, however, she felt obliged to live in Warsaw, he was ready to join her there, to forget his physics, and teach French for a living. It was impossible for Marie to allow such a sacrifice, and impossible for her to hold out against him any longer.

'It is sad that I must stay in Paris for ever,' she wrote to an old Polish friend, 'but what am I to do? Fate has made us deeply attached to each other, and we cannot endure the idea of separating.'

She was engaged to Pierre when she went back to Paris, and on 23 July 1895 they were married in Sceaux. Neither of them wanted a church wedding, nor any kind of fuss. Instead of a wedding dress, Marie wore a navy-blue woollen suit which would do for working in the laboratory afterwards.

As soon as the wedding was over, they set off on bicycles for their honeymoon. Ahead seemed to stretch blissful years in which they could study and discuss physics together.

6 The Mysterious Rays

The Curies rented a three-roomed flat. There was not much furniture because Marie hated dusting, and the meals were terrible. She found boiling a pan of beans far more difficult than any scientific experiment. But food and possessions were not important to Marie and Pierre. Their real life was in the laboratory. Pierre continued his research on magnetism; Marie published the results of her research on steel. They were very happy, and when their first daughter, Irene, was born in 1897, Marie thankfully left the care of her to Pierre's father, who had come to live with them.

She had decided to work for the advanced degree of Doctor of Science, and by 1897 she was looking for a new subject to research. Very recently a scientist called Henri Becquerel had discovered that urianium salts spontaneously gave off rays of an unknown nature. The mystery of the rays fascinated Marie. What caused them? What could they do? With Pierre's encouragement, she chose the uranium rays for her research subject.

Because the Sorbonne could not offer her any room, she started her work in an unused laboratory at Pierre's School of Physics and Chemistry. It would have been hard to find anywhere less suitable for important scientific research. The tiny, badly-equipped laboratory was bakingly hot in summer, and in winter cold and damp enough to interfere with her precision instruments. But after her attic years, unfavourable conditions did not worry Marie, and she plunged excitedly into

Henri Becquerel

her experiments.

She soon discovered that the rays given off by uranium were very unusual. She examined them in conditions of heat, light, wetness and darkness, and nothing seemed to affect them. She compared other elements with uranium, and found that only one, thorium, gave out similar rays, and was thus — to use the term she invented — radioactive.

As her experiments continued, it began to seem that some minerals containing uranium were more radioactive than she would have expected. Could they include another, as yet unidentified, element, more strongly radioactive than uranium? When Marie

40

mentioned this theory to other physicists, they refused to believe her. Scornfully they told her that all the scientific elements were known already. Was it likely that a woman — a woman! — had found a new one? But Marie would not change her mind. She knew what she had proved in her odd little laboratory; and in April 1898 she announced, in a scientific magazine, that pitch-blende — a mineral which included uranium — certainly also contained a powerfully radioactive, and previously undiscovered, element.

She now had to prove her theory by isolating the new element. It was a daunting task, but Marie was no longer working alone. Pierre, who had followed her experiments with enormous interest, abandoned his own research to help her. They worked side by side, jotting down their observations in the same notebook. By chemical means they analysed the pitch-blende, and found to their surprise that it contained *two* new elements — one which Marie called polonium, in honour of Poland, and another, stronger element, extraordinarily radioactive, which they called radium.

The other scientists remained doubtful. The elements isolated by the Curies were in such minute traces they could barely be said to exist at all. Marie and Pierre knew they must produce them in large enough quantities to overcome disbelief. To do this they would need to acquire and treat a considerable mass of pitch-blende.

A genius is said to be a person with an infinite capacity for taking pains. If the definition is correct, Marie showed herself to be a genius now. She was determined to prove, beyond a shadow of doubt, the existence of radium, and she did not mind how long or how hard she had to work to do so. Searching for a cheap source of pitch-blende, because they had very little money, she remembered that it was mined in the pine forests of Austria, and the uranium taken out for making glass. The waste pitch-blende, left after the uranium had been extracted, could be just what she needed; and with the help of an Austrian colleague, she managed to get a tonne, free of charge.

Sacks of it arrived one day at the laboratory on a coal wagon, a dusty brown mineral mixed with pine needles from the forest where it had been mined. There was far too much for the laboratory to hold. But across the yard was a little wooden shed, even more primitive than the laboratory, and here the gigantic task was begun.

'It was in that miserable old shed,' Marie wrote, 'that the best and happiest days of our life were spent, entirely consecrated to work.'

Outside in the yard, with a cauldron slung over a fire, Marie smelted down the pitch-blende, twenty kilograms at a time. She worked in a dirty, acid-stained overall, stirring the boiling mass with an iron rod. In the shed Pierre analysed the mineral extracts she obtained. They talked endlessly about the wonderful, powerful element they would isolate.

'What will it be like?' Marie asked; and Pierre answered, 'I should like it to have a very beautiful colour.'

Month after month the work went on. When the smelting was at last finished, Marie joined Pierre at his

Marie smelting pitch-blende

analysis in the shed. Its old wooden tables were loaded with more and more concentrated solutions of radium. But as, enthralled, they studied their new element, they failed to realize a most important thing. Its mysterious rays were extremely harmful to human beings.

Handling it constantly, breathing in its gas, Marie and Pierre began to suffer from its secret effects. Marie's fingers were painfully burned. Pierre ached all over, as if he had rheumatism. They were tired. They took a long time to recover from minor coughs and colds. Yet they never connected their ailments with radioactivity. For years they had been indifferent to their own comfort, and they were still the same. They seldom took a break. They gulped down inadequate meals so as not to waste time, not caring how thin they became. Often they ate in the shed, unaware that the radium-laden atmosphere was contaminating even their sandwiches.

Sometimes, when they had finished work and gone home, the fascination of the radium would draw them back. They had been working on it for four years, and the new element was in its most concentrated form, when, just before bedtime one night, Marie suggested to Pierre a last visit to the shed. They hurried through the dim Paris streets, and Pierre put his key into the shed door.

'Don't light the lamp for a minute,' whispered Marie. 'Do you remember how you wished that radium was a beautiful colour?'

As the door swung back, they saw that Pierre's wish had come true. All round the shed the glass tubes of radium shone through the darkness, with a strange, blue, phosphorescent glow.

7   Radium

'Working in a shed might sound romantic,' Marie wrote, long after the discovery of radium had made her famous, 'but the romantic element was not an advantage. It wore out our strength, and delayed our accomplishment.'

The poor conditions in the shed put extra stress on two people already weakened by exposure to radiation. It was always cold, the floor was trodden earth, plaster flaked from the ceiling, the tap dripped. Only scientists as utterly dedicated as Marie and Pierre could have persevered with their research in such surroundings; and they were human enough to feel resentment at times, and long for a better laboratory.

If only, Marie sometimes reflected sadly, Pierre's brilliance was recognized, he might be offered a new job, with access to a well-equipped laboratory. The Sorbonne should have made him a professor, but people who wanted academic posts were supposed to go humbly round their colleagues begging for support, and Pierre refused to do this. He knew that, with such a system, good positions went, not to those who deserved them, but to those who were best at currying favour. He wanted the university simply to acknowledge the value of his work, and this they did not do. The French government, in 1902, actually offered him their highest decoration, the Legion of Honour, for his contribution to French science, but Pierre turned it down. 'I do not feel the slightest need of being decorated,' he wrote, 'but I am in the greatest need of a laboratory.' Still the

Teaching physics at the girl's school

academic world ignored him.

The Curies were always short of money. Marie had no salary or grant, and Pierre's salary was so low that it was quickly swallowed up by their living expenses, and by the wages of the maid and nurse, who looked after the house and little Irene. There was none to spare for advancing their research, and so, to earn a bit more, Marie took a job in a girls' school, where she taught physics two days a week. She was an excellent teacher, one of the first to allow her pupils to try practical experiments. More importantly, the work gave her a regular break from the contaminated atmosphere of the shed — something which Pierre never had. But Marie did not realize her good fortune. She only grumbled at the time she wasted in preparing her lessons, teaching, and travelling to and fro.

Still the research went on; still it was their supreme preoccupation. Between 1899 and 1904 Marie and Pierre published thirty-two articles about their work. Their discovery of a new, exciting element could no longer be doubted, and mounting interest in radio-activity spread throughout the scientific world. An elderly professor, who had followed their reports, was warned by his doctor that he had not long to live. 'I can't die yet!' he exclaimed crossly. 'I want to know more about radium.'

Not only was radium gaining recognition as a vitally important new element by scientists in the new field of atomic physics. Ordinary people, who read simplified accounts of the discovery in their newspapers, were fascinated as well. The knowledge that their work was arousing such interest spurred the Curies on. Nothing but radium mattered. When a friend suggested that they might relax occasionally, and even eat a meal without talking about physics the whole time, Marie and Pierre took no notice.

In March 1902 they achieved their long-awaited goal. There in the shed, in a glass tube, were crystals of pure radium, made from the pitch-blende, and visible to human eyes for the first time. Radium looked like ordinary salt, but it was a million times more radioactive

The first crystals of pure radium

than uranium. Marie and Pierre discovered that its rays penetrated every mineral except lead. For their own sake they should, from then on, have worked with the radium in lead containers, but that would have taken time and money which they could not spare. It was much easier and cheaper to go on using ordinary glass containers, even though their hands were often burned through the glass. They did not understand the seriousness of the burns. Pierre, indeed, burned his own arm deliberately, and recorded the developing stages of the injury with scientific detachment. It had certainly not occurred to them that everything in the shed, from the tables to the dust in the atmosphere, was becoming radioactive. Eighty-five years later their notebooks are still too dangerous to be handled without precautions.

In 1903 Marie submitted an account of her work for her doctor's degree. She called it *Researches on Radioactive Substances* by Madame Sklodovska-Curie. The examiners summoned her, as was the custom, to appear in public, and be questioned about it.

The new black dress, which Bronya persuaded her to buy, was Marie's only concession to the drama of the occasion. It was right, she thought, to give a dry, factual description of her discoveries; and although an excited audience filled the hall, Marie took no notice of them, but sat facing the examiners, with her burned hands and untidy hair, explaining her work in the most matter-of-fact way, sometimes pausing to sketch a diagram on the blackboard. But her flat words could not quench the universal enthusiasm. She was awarded her degree, with the citation 'very honourable'.

Before publishing her results, Marie had taken time to consider what she was doing. If she patented her technique for treating pitch-blende, other people who followed her method of producing radium would have to pay for the right to do so. The Curies could have become rich; rich enough to build a proper laboratory. Tempting though the idea was, Marie rejected it. To profit financially from a discovery was contrary to the disinterested scientific spirit in which she and Pierre had always tried to work.

But by now the Curies were winning recognition, and even fame. There were both genuine scientists and celebrity-hunters in the audience which attended a lecture given by Pierre at London's Royal Institute. As he pulled a glass tube of radium from his pocket, the New Zealand physicist, Ernest Rutherford, noticed the terrible marks on his hands. He noticed, too, that Pierre spilled a few grains — fifty years later the room was still so radioactive it needed decontaminating. Pierre noticed neither the tiny mishap, nor his own familiar burns. He was calculating how many laboratories could be bought with the jewellery worn by the ladies in the audience.

Six months later the Curies were awarded the Nobel Prize for Physics, one of the greatest honours in the scientific world. Suddenly, everyone was talking about them. Journalists besieged the shed, and mail arrived by the sackful, with letters of congratulation, requests for autographs, even poems praising radium. Pierre and Marie had no idea how to cope with the publicity. Although they knew their results would interest other scientists, they had never imagined such an outcry in the popular press, such a demand for interviews and photographs. They hated being hailed as superstars; that was not what science was about. They were dedicated to the advancement of knowledge, not the advancement of the Curies. When Marie was recognized in the street, she refused to admit her identity. More and more she and Pierre withdrew from the world, shutting themselves up amongst the still unsuspected dangers of their shed.

For it was dangerous. Neither Marie nor Pierre was well enough to go to Sweden to receive the prize. Pierre was particularly ill, with such pains in his body and limbs that for days he could only stay in bed.

Ironically, the burning of his arm had been part of an investigation into the biological effects of radium. Since it could destroy body cells, he began, with some medical friends, to consider if it could be used to treat cancer. The idea that radium could burn away diseased cells was greeted with enthusiasm. Experiments were tried with mice; and, in the last scientific paper he wrote, Pierre mentioned that a side effect of the radium on them was the destruction of their white blood

Pierre studying the side-effects of radium

corpuscles. It will never be known if Pierre thought of applying this chance discovery to human beings, especially to himself and Marie. Was he too tired and limp to inquire if radioactivity could be destroying *their* white corpuscles — the element in the blood that fights infection? Or did he guess the truth, and keep it to himself?

Life should have been improving for the Curies. Not only were they enriched by their prize money, but their ordinary income had soared. At last Pierre had been made a professor at the Sorbonne, with Marie appointed as his chief laboratory assistant. In their new laboratory they tackled the tough problem of measuring the emanation of radium. At home there was a new baby, Eva. But nothing could be properly enjoyed — not as those early days in the shed had been enjoyed. They were exhausted, and Pierre was depressed too. He had begun to have nightmare visions of what might happen if radium got into criminal hands. And could it somehow be used in warfare? He almost wished Marie had never discovered her new element.

Marie was very worried about him. He had changed from an eager scientist into a weary pessimist. He looked thin and ill. But if anything happened to him, how could she go on? She depended on him so much.

'Pierre,' she said one day, 'if one of us' (she meant him) 'disappeared, the other could not survive.'

For the last time Pierre roused himself to defend his old ideals.

'You are wrong,' he answered. 'Whatever happens, a scientist's work must go on.'

8 Accident in a Paris Street

On Thursday, 19 April 1906, Marie and Pierre awoke to the sound of rain pattering down. They spent the morning as usual in the laboratory, and then Pierre set off under his umbrella to join the other professors of science for lunch. He left them at about half past two, and walked on to the offices of his publisher, whom he wanted to see before returning to his work. But a strike had closed the place down, so, putting up his umbrella against the heavy rain, Pierre turned away.

He was in an old, overcrowded part of Paris. The street was so narrow that two lines of traffic could hardly pass. Walkers found it difficult to make progress, and spilled from the pavement into the gutters. That was what Pierre did. He walked along in the roadway, following a horsedrawn cab.

Along the street, the Rue Dauphine, he went, towards the river Seine. Before he reached the bridge he had to cross a main road, thronged with traffic. As a tram went clanging by, a huge, heavy wagon cut in front of it, and dashed into the Rue Dauphine at a fast pace, with the driver fighting to control his horses. At that moment Pierre moved out from behind the cab to cross the road. Before he could step back, the wagon was upon him. The horses plunged, striking out with their hooves. Pierre fell, and the wagon wheels passed right over him.

Those were the facts of the accident, but what had been the real cause? Why had Pierre launched himself so heedlessly into the traffic? Was he feeling too ill to know what he was doing? Had the cab, or the umbrella, blocked his view? Was he so lost in thought that he failed to notice the noise of the wagon approaching, although other people heard the din it was making? Was it even possible that, depressed and disenchanted as he was with radium, he had half meant to end his life?

For end it, he did. There was no hope of reviving the body which was picked up from the street, and carried to the police station. Papers in his pocket revealed his identity; and two professors, summoned from the Sorbonne, were asked to break the news to Marie.

She had not got back from the laboratory when they arrived at the Curies' house. Only Pierre's father was there. 'What was he thinking of this time?' he asked despairingly, but nobody could answer that. At six o'clock Marie came in, and, as gently as they could, the professors told her what had happened. They were prepared for screams, cries or fainting fits, but there were none. Marie stood, white and motionless, without speaking. Then she turned away, and walking out into the garden, she sat down alone under the wet trees.

No one knew what she was thinking. Perhaps she was remembering the fair at Sceaux, the moment when she and Pierre were swept apart, and Pierre had the premonition that, just as suddenly, their relationship would end — as it had done. Even when Pierre's body was brought to the house, she did not weep. Indeed she seemed to have been struck dumb. She only managed to tell the children that their father had been badly hurt, and she hardly spoke to the sympathetic callers, or even to Bronya who was soon at her side.

The funeral was on Saturday. Crowds gathered; messages poured in from kings, scientists and ordinary people. At last, in brief, unemotional words, Marie told Irene and Eva that their father was dead.

On Sunday, after a sleepless night, Marie went back to the laboratory. She set up the apparatus for measuring radium emanations, and opened her notebook at the graph she and Pierre had been making together. But the sight of his writing overcame her. She shut the book, and put it away. It seemed impossible to go on without him.

Days, weeks passed. Only to Bronya could Marie pour out even a fraction of the grief, rage and bitterness that tormented her. Only large, motherly Bronya could hold thin, brittle Marie in her arms, and attempt to comfort her. Marie kept her other acquaintances at a distance. They knew nothing of her sufferings, of the tortured diary she kept at this time, or of the terrible night when she nerved herself to burn Pierre's bloodstained clothes.

But Pierre had said that a scientist's work must go on; and presently Marie found that work was, after all, the best help. All through the day, and on into the night, she stayed in the laboratory, observing, purifying, measuring radium. Gradually it returned to its old place at the centre of her life.

The effect of Pierre's death was not so much to change Marie, as to make her more concentratedly herself. Because she could not remember receiving gestures of love from her mother, she found it difficult to express

Marie alone with her grief

love for her own children. Now she kept more aloof from them than ever. She never spoke to them about their father; she could not bear to pronounce his name. She would not weep; she rejected pity; and when she was not working, she would sit gazing into space, rubbing her sore, burned fingers together.

Less than a month after Pierre's death, the university authorities asked Marie if she would take his old job as professor of physics. She was the first woman to be offered such a position, but she felt no pleasure, and little interest. 'I will try it,' she answered flatly. Nevertheless the news caused a stir; and when the university year began in November, the physics lecture hall was packed with professors, students, and even society ladies in large hats, eager to hear Professor Marie Curie's first lecture. In such circumstances the lecturer normally began by paying tribute to his, or her, predecessor. What would Marie say about Pierre? The crowd waited, agog.

At 1.30 Marie entered the hall to a storm of applause. She bowed her head, and waited for silence. The atmosphere was tense. 'When one considers the progress made in physics in the last ten years,' she began drily, 'one finds an advance in our ideas about electricity.' And she went on, quite impersonally, to describe the structure of electricity, picking up the threads of Pierre's course without a single reference to him. The society ladies drooped with boredom.

The hour's lecture ended. Would this be the moment for the tribute? But no. Still frozen-faced, Marie gathered up her papers, and left the hall, while the audience rose slowly to their feet, frustrated and disappointed.

9 The Lonely Scientist

From the early days when little Marya Sklodovska astonished her family with her powers of concentration, hard work had been Marie's habit, and nothing could change it now. Radium still fascinated her, and in the years after Pierre's death she went tirelessly on with her experiments. She measured its atomic weight, she prepared a Radium Standard by which its purity could be assessed, and finally, by distilling and condensing radium chloride in a most difficult scientific operation, she produced tiny, but recognizable, specks of a shiny white metal which was radium itself. She published many books and articles about her researches, and in 1911 she won the Nobel Prize for Chemistry, being the first person to receive two Nobel Prizes.

Outwardly her life seemed prosperous. As a professor of physics she was at last given a good salary, and a proper laboratory to work in. She had an international reputation as a scientist. But real happiness had gone for ever when the wagon wheels crushed Pierre. She was lost without him.

Pierre had always contributed the human qualities to their marriage. Perhaps because his childhood had been easier than Marie's, his personality was warmer than hers. She was the accurate mathematician, the indefatigable researcher. He was the one with imagination. Marie loved country activities, but Pierre really loved and understood nature. The study of symmetry which he undertook before he met Marie was the result of his close observation of natural things, like flowers, cobwebs and snowflakes. With his particular intellect it was not surprising that he was the one who saw the frightening implications of their discoveries, and worried about them. Marie found it much harder to link the work of the laboratory with the world outside its walls. Pure science was her lifelong ideal.

From the time when he took his first degree at the age of sixteen, Pierre had been part of the Parisian scientific establishment; yet even so he only received full recognition in the last two years of his life, because he would not adopt the rigid French habit of begging personally for promotion. Marie hated the system just as much, and she had the disadvantages of being a woman and a foreigner. Nevertheless, when she decided in 1910 to seek election to the Academy of Sciences, a society where France's top scientists met for discussions, it was assumed that she would be chosen. France had no more famous scientist than Marie Curie. On the day of the election her laboratory assistants bought a bouquet of flowers to present to her when the results were announced. They were shattered to learn that the Academy had voted against her. The bouquet was hidden under the bench, and Marie, deeply wounded, continued her studies in solitude.

Her youthful plumpness had disappeared long ago. Now she was thin, with a pale face set in harsh lines of disappointment. Her cold manner and black clothes put people off. Yet inwardly she was painfully vulnerable, as the shock of her rejection by the Academy showed. She was frequently ill too, with vague aches and pains, exhaustion, kidney problems, and anaemia. Never, for one moment, would she connect these complaints with radium. She worked on, refusing to lighten her load.

But there were some good moments — in July 1914, for example, when a cherished dream came true. A Radium Institute was opened in Paris, where, under Marie's direction, all aspects of radioactivity could be studied, from methods of treating cancer to the purely experimental work which was still closest to Marie's heart.

There was no time to enjoy the Radium Institute before the First World War broke out. As the Germans advanced into northern France and Belgium, Marie looked for a way of using her scientific knowledge to help her adopted country. She quickly found one. Twenty years earlier X-rays had been discovered by a physicist called Wilhelm Röntgen, and X-rays, since they involved radiation, were of great interest to Marie. They were not frequently used by doctors, but Marie saw how valuable they could be.

Immediately she devised what she called a 'radiological car'. Into the car she packed lightweight X-ray equipment which could be powered by the car's motor, and, with a chauffeur to drive, she set off for the battlefront. War casualties were flooding into the military hospitals, and Marie's help was welcomed eagerly. At each hospital she chose a suitable room and set up her equipment, while the chauffeur unrolled the electric cable, and connected it to the engine. As the injured soldiers were carried in, Marie focussed her camera on their wounds, sometimes taking photographs, some-

60

The radiological car

times throwing a picture onto a screen to guide the surgeon's operations.

This was Marie's work throughout the war. When it finished she had been responsible for equipping two hundred radiological units. She had organized the training of groups of girl assistants, including her daughter Irene. She had learned to drive, in case she had to manage without a chauffeur. Most importantly of all, she had proved the value of X-rays.

There was a price to pay. The rudimentary precautions she took against radiation — the gloves and overall she wore for work, the care she took not to stand directly in the X-ray beam — were not enough. When the war ended she was not only weak and ill. She was going blind.

Today cataract, a disease which causes blindness, is known as one of the symptoms of exposure to radiation. In 1918 nobody, least of all Marie, believed that radium could damage eyes. Back in the Radium Institute, she refused to acknowledge that anything was wrong. She printed her lecture notes in enormous letters, and painted coloured signs on her instrument dials, to hide her disability. 'I couldn't live without my laboratory,' she told Bronya. Nor, although she did not say this, could she have lived without her single-minded love and trust for radium.

In due course several operations restored her sight. She travelled abroad as a famous personality, and continued her work at the Institute. But inexorably evidence against radium mounted. It was a double-edged tool, valuable for destroying the diseased cells of cancer patients, but attacking healthy cells as well.

For years Marie was amazingly resistant to the effects of radiation. She absorbed far more than most people could survive. Her resistance encouraged her to shut her eyes to its dangers. When workers in her laboratory died of leukaemia, she merely commented that they had not taken enough fresh air.

In the summer of 1934 she at last collapsed with leukaemia herself. She was rushed to a mountain hospital, where various comforting diagnoses were offered. She might be suffering from gallstones, or perhaps tuberculosis. No one said that the radium had finally contaminated even her blood.

As she lay dying, her confused mind kept turning back to her work. 'Yogurt?' she murmured, as the nurse tried to help her to eat. 'Has it been made with radium or mesothorium?'

Her daughters and son-in-law were at her bedside when she died on 4 July 1934. They carried her body back to Sceaux, and buried her beside Pierre.